David Thompson

Battle of the Monkey And the Crab

David Thompson

Battle of the Monkey And the Crab

ISBN/EAN: 9783744704199

Printed in Europe, USA, Canada, Australia, Japan

Cover: Foto ©Thomas Meinert / pixelio.de

More available books at **www.hansebooks.com**

Published by the Kobunsha, 2, Minami Saegicho, Tokyo.

日本昔噺第三號

再版 猿蟹合戰

定價金十二錢

米國 ダビッドタムソン先生 譯

日本 鮮齋永濯 畵

明治十八年八月十七日 版權免許

同 十九年九月廿九日 添題御届

同 十一月二日 再版御届

出版所

東京南佐柄木町二番地

弘文社

BATTLE

OF

THE MONKEY & THE CRAB.

A monkey and a crab once met when going round a mountain.

The monkey had picked up a persimmon-seed, and the crab had a piece of toasted rice-cake. The monkey seeing this, and wishing to get something that could be turned to good account at once, said: "Pray, exchange that rice-cake for this persimmon-seed." The crab, without a word, gave up his cake, and took the persimmon-seed and planted it. At

once it sprung up, and soon became a tree so high one had to
look up at it. The tree was full
of persimmons but the crab had
no means of climbing the tree.
So he asked the monkey to climb
up and get the persimmons for him.
The monkey got up on a limb
of the tree and began to eat the
persimmons. The unripe persimmons he threw at the crab, but

all the ripe and good ones he put in his pouch. The crab under the tree thus got his shell badly bruised and only by good luck escaped into his hole, where he lay distressed with pain and not able to get up. Now when the relatives and household of the crab heard how matters stood they were surprised and angry, and declared war and attacked the

monkey, who leading forth a nu-
merous following bid defiance to
the other party. The crabs, find-
ing themselves unable to meet and

cope with this force, became still more ex-

asperated and enraged, and retreated into

their hole, and held a council of war.

Then came a rice-mortar, a pounder, a bee, and an egg, and together they devised a deep-laid plot to be avenged.

First, they requested that peace be made with the crabs; and thus they induced the king of the monkeys to enter their hole unattended, and seated him on the hearth. The monkey not suspecting any

plot, took the *hibashi*, or poker, to
stir up the slumbering fire, when
bang! went the egg, which was
lying hidden in the ashes, and
burned the monkey's arm.   Surprised and alarmed he plunged

his arm into the pickle-tub in the kitchen to relieve the pain of the burn. Then the bee which was hidden near the tub stung him sharply in his face already wet with tears. Without waiting to brush

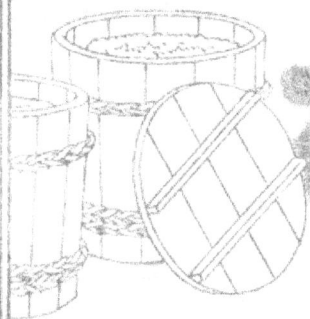

off the bee and howling bitterly, he rushed for the back door: but just then some sea-weed entangled his legs and made him slip. Then, down came the pounder tumbling on him from a shelf, and the mortar too came rolling down on him from the roof of the porch, and broke his back and so weakened him that he was unable to rise up. Then

out came the crabs in a crowd
and brandishing on high their
pinchers they pinched the monkey
to pieces.